ROLLING A KAYAK

BY KEN WHITING

ROLLING A KAYAK

BY KEN WHITING

THE HELICONIA PRESS

Published by

 THE **HELICONIA PRESS**

1576 Beachburg Road
Beachburg, Ontario K0J 1C0
www.helipress.com

This book was printed in Singapore

First Edition

ISBN # 978-1-896980-27-0

Written by: Ken Whiting
Photography by: Paul Villecourt
Illustrations by: Paul Mason
Design and Layout: Robyn Hader
Edited by: Rebecca Sandiford

Library and Archives Canada Cataloguing in Publication

Whiting, Ken, 1974-

Rolling a kayak, with Ken Whiting / author, Ken Whiting ; editor,
Rebecca Sandiford ; photography, Paul Villecourt ; illustrator, Paul Mason.

Includes index.
ISBN 978-1-896980-27-0

1. Kayaking-Safety measures. 2. Kayaking-Training.
I. Sandiford, Rebecca, 1973- II. Title.

GV784.55.W54 2007   797.122'40289   C2006-905479-7

About Safety

Kayaking is an activity with inherent risks, and this book is designed as a general guide, not a substitute for experience. The publisher and the author do not take responsibility for the use of any of the materials or methods described in this book. By following any of the procedures described within, you do so at your own risk.

TABLE OF CONTENTS

INTRODUCTION TO THE KAYAK ROLL

"All experts were once beginners!" (Tyler Curtis)

One of the greatest things about kayaking is that, as a sport, it has something to offer everyone. For many, kayaking is simply a means of getting some exercise in the outdoors, but for a growing number of people, kayaking is a sport that provides the excitement of almost continuously learning new skills, refining techniques, and the satisfaction of making progress over time. For this latter group, there are some great reasons to take the time to learn to roll, and I can assure you that it will be worth your effort.

For whitewater kayakers, rolling is an important skill to master. Knowing how to roll doesn't mean you won't swim every once in a while, because sometimes you won't have a choice; but swimming should be your last resort. Aside from being tiring, frightening, and humbling, you're much more vulnerable to hazards when swimming in whitewater. A reliable roll is also a great confidence-builder, which means you'll be more relaxed on the water and more inclined to try new things. Invariably, this results in a steeper learning curve.

Although rolling is not an essential skill for touring and sea kayakers, there's no question that a reliable roll is a huge asset for many of the same reasons that it's good for whitewater paddlers to learn: it lets you paddle more safely, helps you be more relaxed on the water, and you'll find your increased confidence will support you in exploring new elements of the sport.

These are some pretty compelling reasons to learn to roll, and the fact that you're reading this probably means that you're interested in doing so. Are there any limitations to who can learn? Unless you're allergic to getting your head wet, you'll be happy to hear that that any reasonably fit paddler can learn to roll, because rolling relies on good technique, not power.

The kayak roll comes in a number of forms. In fact, taking into account all of the Greenland kayak roll variations, there are over 100 types of rolls that one could learn. Practically though, most paddlers only need to consider one roll; the one that will get them upright! In this book, we're going to focus on what most instructors would consider the most common and important types of rolls. We'll start by looking at the fundamental techniques and concepts that need to be understood for any of these rolls to be performed competently and safely. We'll then look at the rolls themselves, along with some of the most common problems people have with them and their solutions. We'll end by looking at real world applications of the rolls, as well as some tricks for teaching the roll.

Let me finish by saying that the roll has been analyzed by more people, and in more depth, than any other kayaking skill. This book deals with techniques and concepts that have been time-tested and proven and that I have learned over the years through teaching, by working with other instructors, and by practical use. There is no single "correct" way to learn to roll. This is not the only way; this is just my way.

Learning to roll will open the doors to new kayaking opportunities and adventures, such as paddling in Chile's spectacular Patagonia region (www.kayakfu.com)

ABOUT THE AUTHOR

Through the 1990's, Ken became one of the most recognized and respected whitewater athletes in the world. Ken was the 1997/98 World Freestyle Kayaking Champion, the 1998 Japan Open Champion, and a five-time National Champion. After winning the World Freestyle Kayaking Championships in 1997, Ken began to focus his passion for paddling on the development of instructional tools. Ken is now one of the most influential paddlers in the world, and was recognized as such by Paddler Magazine as one of their "Paddlers of the Century." He has paddled on over 200 rivers in 15 countries and has ten best-selling, award-winning instructional books and DVDs to his name. Ken has also co-founded an industry-leading kayak school, and an adventure kayaking travel company with a base camp in Chile's Patagonia region. Ken and his wife Nicole live in Beachburg, Canada, where they run their publishing business - The Heliconia Press. For more information, visit www.helipress.com

HOW AND WHERE TO LEARN

Over the years, I've had the great fortune (and occasional amusement) of watching people learn in such very different ways. Although most people require the direct help of an instructor, I've watched some first time paddlers flip and roll right back up unassisted, having only watched someone perform the roll beforehand. Although a few people have an uncanny ability to pick up the roll, as a general rule the best way to learn the roll is with professional instruction in a controlled, warm water environment (such as a beach or an indoor pool). Not only can a good instructor teach you to roll the most quickly, but they will help make sure that you learn to do it in the safest way. An unfortunate reality about kayaking is that the shoulder dislocation is a relatively common injury—in the same way that a torn ACL (knee ligament) is common for skiers—and the roll is one of the more common ways for this to happen. Most paddling schools or clubs will host rolling clinics throughout the year. The winter is a great time to polish your skills so that you're ready to go when spring arrives.

Although professional instruction is the ideal solution for learning the roll, the reality is that many people get involved with kayaking thanks to the encouragement and guidance of their friends, who are also relied upon for instruction. I don't mean to discount your friend as a viable instructor, but it is important to realize that teaching is a very different skill than performing. As a case in point, it is not a valid assumption that the best paddlers in the world are the best teachers. The best teachers are the best communicators. If you plan on learning from your friends or even on your own with only the help of this book, I don't want to discourage you from doing so. My advice would be to make sure you learn the right technique. Not only will you help prevent injury, but bad habits only get harder to break over time.

CHAPTER 1

photo: Jock Bradley

EQUIPMENT

KAYAK

PADDLE

SPRAY SKIRT

PERSONAL FLOTATION DEVICE

OTHER LEARNING AIDS

When learning to roll, the equipment that you use will have a significant bearing on your success. This doesn't mean that in order to roll, you'll need to go out and spend a small fortune on a new set of "rolling" equipment, but you do need equipment that fits you, and you may want to borrow or rent a piece of gear or two. The simple truth about learning any new skill is that the first few attempts are always the most difficult. I recommend taking advantage of any opportunity that might make reaching your goal easier.

Although your body isn't something that you'd normally refer to as a piece of equipment, your body is your most important tool, and although rolling is a skill that relies on good technique—not on power—a strong, healthy and flexible body will only be helpful for learning. In particular, flexibility is an asset and some people are surprised to hear that lower body flexibility is just as important to develop as upper body flexibility. Tight hips will impede your ability to roll the kayak on edge, and tight hamstrings can dramatically affect your ability to lean forward.

As we all know, flexibility is something that seems to take much longer to gain than to lose. The key to developing or maintaining flexibility is to make stretching a part of your weekly routine. And of course, before launching yourself into a major rolling lesson, take the time to warm up and stretch.

KAYAK

Although it is possible to roll virtually any kayak with the right technique, there are some features that make some kayaks easier to roll than others. But the biggest issue affecting a kayak's "rollability" doesn't actually have to do with the boat's shape; it has to do with the outfitting inside the kayak. This is what we're going to look at first.

OUTFITTING

A kayak should fit like a good pair of shoes—snug yet comfortable. Imagine trying to rock climb, ski, or hike in simple rubber boots, four sizes too big for your feet. This

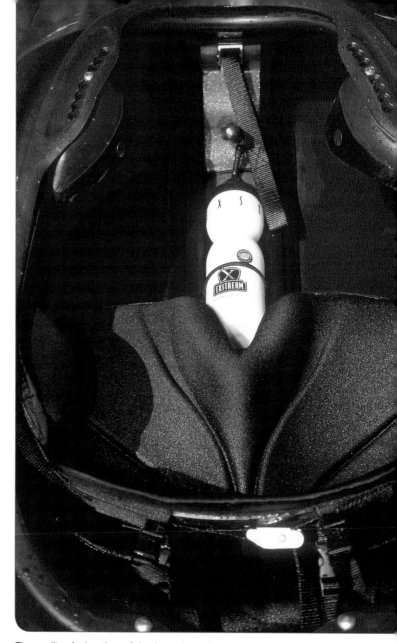

The quality of a boat's outfitting has a huge impact on the ease with which it can be rolled.

is exactly what kayaking in an incorrectly outfitted kayak can be like. Not only will your performance be seriously compromised, but your comfort will also suffer. Thankfully, manufacturers have acknowledged the need for a good fit in a kayak and have developed outfitting systems that can be easily customized. If you're lucky, it will only take a few small adjustments before your kayak is ready to go.

Having emphasized the need for a snug and comfortable fit, it's equally important to note that you should never, under any circumstances, do anything that will impede your ability to wet-exit a kayak or to easily re-enter it from the water.

Before looking at specific outfitting, let's start by looking at how you should be sitting in your kayak. We'll then work backwards and look at how you can outfit your kayak to promote the proper position.

When sitting in your kayak, your legs should be in front of you with your knees bent and legs splayed out and under the thigh hooks. Your feet should be resting comfortably against their supports. When sitting upright like this on the water, your kayak should be "trimmed out", which means that the bow and stern should be out of the water equally. Trimming is of greater concern for whitewater kayaks, which are much

shorter than their sea kayak brethren. If you find your stern is lower in the water, you'll need to move yourself forward in your kayak by sliding the seat forward and/or tightening the back band slightly. If you find your bow is lower in the water, or that you are short on foot room, you will need to move the seat backwards slightly or loosen the back band.

Now that you're sitting in your kayak correctly, let's look at how you can outfit your kayak to fit like a pair of good shoes. When outfitting a kayak, you need to consider the support that is provided to your feet, legs, butt, hips, and lower back.

FOOT SUPPORTS

Depending on the type and model of your kayak, it will have foot pegs, or a movable bulkhead, or a foam bulkhead system.

Foot pegs are small plates that slide forward and backward along a track to accommodate different leg lengths. These

The ideal sitting position has your knees bent and legs splayed out and under the thigh hooks, while your feet rest comfortably against the foot pegs.

are the most easily adjusted form of foot support and are the standard for sea kayaks. The downside of foot pegs is that sand has a tendency to get caught in the track, making their adjustment more difficult over time.

A movable bulkhead is a wall of plastic that slides forward and backward and then gets locked into place. These are the preferred foot supports for whitewater kayaks for safety reasons unique to river running.

Some whitewater kayaks will have foam bulkheads, which are basically chunks of foam that are stuffed into the bow of the kayak, creating a wall of support for your feet. Foam bulkheads can be quite comfortable and are not a bad option. The downside is that the foam does compress, which means that the fitting will become looser over time and will require adjustments. This compressed foam can also push out the plastic in the bow of your kayak and increase bow volume where you don't need or want it.

OUTFITTING TIP

For padding, closed-cell foam (also referred to as mini-cell foam) is a wonderful material that absorbs no water, is easily shaped, and provides a firm yet pliant surface to press against. To attach foam in place, prepare the surfaces of both the boat and the foam by roughening them with coarse sandpaper, and then use contact cement to glue the pads in. You can then shape the foam to a custom fit with a serrated knife, sandpaper or with a Sureform. Make sure that all your outfitting is secure in the kayak so that when you end up swimming it doesn't all get washed away.

LEG SUPPORT

Your legs should fit comfortably under the thigh hooks with even pressure across your thighs. If your kayak doesn't have thigh hooks, you'll want to get your hands on one that does. The thigh hooks on most recent kayak models can usually be adjusted to fit a wide range of leg girth and length, but older models may not offer this feature and will require some

customized padding. Though it is most important that your thigh hooks provide your legs with a surface to squeeze against for support and to pull up against for edging, it is also very helpful if your legs are supported from the outside and from underneath. This additional support provides supplementary control and helps reduce hip discomfort. Although some whitewater kayak models have outfitting that provides this additional support, there's a good chance that you'll need to add this piece of outfitting yourself, using foam blocks.

BUTT SUPPORT

Your butt may be one of the most padded parts of your body, but this doesn't mean that it won't appreciate a little tender loving care. Many seats now come equipped with seat padding, but if yours doesn't, try gluing a quarter inch of mini-cell foam on your seat to make your time on the water much more comfortable. Some whitewater paddlers who are short in the torso may find it helpful to glue even more foam to their seat to raise their centre of gravity. While for some people, adding foam can provide more control over edging and make it easier to set up for a roll, beware of raising yourself too high. Being too high will make you tippy and potentially decrease your boat control.

BACK SUPPORT

Back support is absolutely critical for both comfort and performance in any type of kayak, and back bands are generally the most functional and effective systems to provide it. The back band should fit above your hips and be tightened enough to prevent you from sliding backwards, but without impeding your ability to lean right back. The best back bands are those held in place with heavy-duty webbing and with rounded hardware that won't create weak points or potentially cut into any of the straps.

HIP SUPPORT

Much of the control you have over your kayak stems from the hips, so it is vital that they are well supported. It's also very important that your hips aren't squeezed too tightly, because

this can cause your legs to fall asleep or just be downright painful. Your hip padding should be snug enough to prevent your butt from sliding from side to side, and no tighter. It's also very helpful if your hip pads cup slightly over your hips and upper thighs, providing some support from above. This provides additional edge control over your kayak and helps keep your butt from falling out of the seat when you are upside-down. Of course, make sure that your hip support still allows an easy escape from the kayak if needed.

BOAT DESIGN

If you've had a chance to paddle a variety of any type of kayak (sea kayak, whitewater kayak, or recreational kayak) you'll know that small differences in boat design can have significant effects on a boat's handling characteristics. This is also true when it comes to rolling. For example, a kayak with a fairly round cross-sectional shape tends to be easier to roll than one with a boxy shape. However, a kayak with a boxy cross-sectional shape won't be noticeably harder to roll if the kayak is a good width for you.

The most important thing to consider when assessing how a boat design will impact its "rollability" is how the boat design fits you personally. As long as a boat doesn't impede your ability to get your upper body out to the side and your paddle to the surface when you're in the set-up phase of your roll, then you shouldn't have a problem. In general, a good set-up position can be difficult in a boat that is too wide for the paddler, or one

The narrowness of a sea kayak makes it easy to get the paddle out of the water and the upper body near the surface during the set-up phase of the roll.

World Squirt Boat Champion, Brendan Mark, uses hockey tape on his paddle for grip and hand positioning.

in which the paddler sits too deeply. The length of both your torso and arms will play a big role in determining what you can get away with.

Basically, any kayak with good outfitting can be rolled—it will just be more difficult if the boat itself doesn't fit you well. Generally, if you're having trouble rolling your kayak, don't sell it, buy a new one, and expect miracles to happen. I'd encourage you instead to start by looking at how you can improve your outfitting. Do you feel as though you're falling out of your kayak when upside-down? Are you having trouble getting your paddle out of the water during your set-up phase? If your outfitting seems fine, I can tell you that there is a 99% chance that your rolling troubles can be traced back to improper technique, not to the kayak that you are using. The good news is, proper technique can be learned.

PADDLE

Because it's possible to roll a kayak without the use of a paddle, it follows that the type of paddle that you use will not greatly impact your ability to roll. However, there are some issues worth considering.

The length of your paddle and the size of its blades do have a small effect on your roll because a longer paddle and bigger blades will provide slightly more support. The feather on your paddle (also known as the "twist", or offset between blade angles), has virtually no effect on your ability to roll in the early stages. All that is important is that you use a paddle with the same twist that you are accustomed to using when just paddling around.

The single best thing that you can do with your paddle to help your rolling is to index the shaft. Indexing the shaft means creating tactile landmarks on your shaft that allow you to maintain or regain the correct grip on your paddle without having to look at it. Most importantly, you'll want to place an index on the "control" handgrip of your paddle. (The control handgrip is where you place the hand that grips the paddle steadily, while the "grease" handgrip is where you place the

Always make sure the ripcord is out when you put on the skirt.

hand that allows the paddle shaft to rotate for each stroke.) The index can be a small strip of foam or wood that is taped to your paddle shaft so that it fits under the fingers of your control hand. Over time, you'll be able to recognize when your hand positioning is off just by the feel of the index. Many paddles now have built-in indexes or oval shafts, which serve the same purpose and are very helpful.

SPRAY SKIRT

The spray skirt (also called a "spray deck") is responsible for sealing off the cockpit of your kayak and keeping water out of your boat. When it comes to practicing rolling, this isn't an optional piece of gear, and the more waterproof your skirt is, the more you'll be able to practice without having to empty out your kayak. Spray skirts are usually made out of either nylon or neoprene, with neoprene being far superior for keeping water out.

All spray skirts have ripcords for pulling the skirt off the boat when you need to get out. Always make sure that the ripcord is out when you put on the skirt. It's also extremely important that you can reliably pop the skirt off the kayak by pulling on the ripcord. If you can't do this comfortably and easily, choose a looser-fitting skirt.

PERSONAL FLOTATION DEVICE

Needless to say, your personal flotation device (PFD) or lifejacket is an essential piece of kayaking equipment, and since you're going to be wearing it at all times on the water, it only makes sense that you wear it when practicing your roll as well.

When choosing a PFD, kayaking-specific models are best because they deliver the flotation you need, in low-profile designs that don't restrict movement. The sizing of your PFD is also important. Your PFD needs to fit snugly and comfortably. If a PFD is too big and loose on your body, it will shift around when you're underwater and can impede your ability to roll.

OTHER LEARNING AIDS

Use nose plugs! There are few things as unpleasant and panic-inducing as the rush of river or pool water up the nose. Aside from being distracting, you'll also blow air from your nose in an attempt to stop the flow of water, which leaves you out of breath sooner and will cause you to rush your roll.

Try a diving mask or goggles. Although I personally don't open my eyes underwater, it can be very helpful for some people to see what they're doing down there. With goggles, you can clearly see if your paddle is positioned properly and then make the required corrections.

A paddle float can be a helpful learning tool. A paddle float attaches to one of your paddle blades and acts like a PFD for your paddle. This allows your paddle to provide more bracing

A paddle float can be a good learning aid. It attaches to the blade of your paddle, and gives it more bracing power.

power and support for a longer time during the roll. The downside of practicing the roll with a paddle float is that you can become too reliant on your paddle. In the execution of a successful roll, other elements are much more important than the paddle, which should really be a minor element.

The paddle float helps keep the active paddle blade near the surface during roll practice. The downside of using a paddle float is that you can become too reliant on your paddle for support and neglect your hip snap.

CHAPTER 2

FUNDAMENTALS

1 *Start the wet exit by leaning forward and yanking the ripcord to pop off your skirt.*

2 *With the skirt popped, slide your hands to your hips, stay leaning forward, and push yourself out of your boat.*

Once you've decided that you're going to learn to roll a kayak, the first order of business is to make sure that you're comfortable underwater. Specifically, you must be completely comfortable with hanging upside-down, underwater, with your lower body sealed in a boat, and you must be confident in your ability to wet exit quickly. With these two conditions met, you'll be in a much better position to give your full attention to learning how to roll. For similar reasons, a warm and controlled environment is the best place to learn your roll, such as an indoor pool or calm, warm-water bay. Although it almost goes without saying, you should also always practice rolling with a buddy around who can assist in getting you and the boat back up should you encounter any unexpected problems.

WET EXIT

A wet exit refers to the act of getting out of your kayak when it's upside-down. The wet exit is the first skill that any paddler should learn.

To exit an overturned kayak smoothly, lean forward and find your skirt's rip cord with one hand, while the other hand firmly hangs on to your paddle. Yank the ripcord forward and up to pop off your skirt. Slide your hands back to your hips, stay leaning forward, and push yourself out of your boat. You'll end up doing a bit of a forward somersault out of the boat. Once you're out of your boat, immediately grab your boat and make sure you still have your paddle. Keeping gear together will greatly speed up the rescue process.

The trickiest part of this maneuver is fighting the instinct to lean back as you slide out of your kayak. The problem with leaning back is that it raises your butt off the seat and presses your thighs against the thigh hooks, which will make it harder to slide out and slow down your wet exit. Leaning back also makes you more vulnerable to underwater rocks when you're upside-down; leaning forward helps protect your face.

The entire process of wet exiting will only take a few seconds, and the more relaxed you are, the more smoothly it'll go. The first few times you try this, it may seem as if you're short of air, but in reality you have lots of time. I recommend that you actually practice sitting there underwater for a few moments before popping out of the boat. This will also help develop your ability to stay calm and collected in a flipped boat.

③ *Roll forward and to the side out of your kayak.*

④ *Try to keep hold of your paddle during the wet exit and then grab your boat as soon as you're out.*

THREE GOLDEN RULES

The "Three Golden Rules" are three key concepts that must be applied during any paddling activity. You must have a co-operative division of your body, you must maintain a power position with your arms, and you must harness the power of torso rotation. These three rules apply to rolling a kayak, as well as any other whitewater, recreational, or sea kayaking technique or stroke. Let's have a closer look...

#1 USE CO-OPERATIVE DIVISION OF THE BODY

The co-operative division of the body is just a fancy way of saying that while your upper body performs one task, your lower body performs a totally separate one. This means there needs to be a distinct separation of upper and lower body movement at the hips. During your roll, the co-operative division of the body allows you to perform the all-important hip snap and also governs your forward and backward leans.

A distinct separation of upper and lower body movements is essential for any form of kayaking.

#2 MAINTAIN THE POWER POSITION

Kayaking is generally a very safe sport, but unfortunately injuries do still occur. The most common injuries are minor ones that stem from overuse, like blisters or tendonitis. But shoulder dislocation is not all that unusual and rolling a kayak has the potential to put your shoulder in a position of risk. To keep your shoulders safe, you need to maintain a power position with your arms.

The power position, in simplest terms, just means keeping your hands in front of your body. If one of your hands gets behind you, it puts your shoulder and arm in a very vulnerable position.

To visualize the power position, imagine looking at your body viewed from above, with an invisible line passing through both shoulders. Let's call this the 'shoulder line". Now imagine another line that divides your body into two equal halves, and call it the "midline". The power position simply involves keeping your hands in front of your shoulder line, and not letting your hands cross your midline. Picture your arms, chest and paddle forming a box when your paddle is held out in front of you. This box is the cornerstone of the power position, and should be maintained at all times. With this rectangle formed, you get the most power from your paddle, and your shoulders stay in the safest position.

Does this mean that you can't reach to the back of your boat to take a stroke? Not at all! It simply means that to do so, you must rotate your whole upper body so that your hands stay in front of you. This brings us to the third rule: torso rotation. Using the power position in combination with torso rotation is critical to a successful and shoulder-safe roll.

During the back deck roll, all three Golden Rules are applied: the upper and lower body work co-operatively but separately, the power position is maintained, and the torso is rotated aggressively.

The back deck roll demonstrates one example of how much torso rotation is used and how the power position is maintained when rolling.

#3 ROTATE YOUR TORSO

Rotating your torso, already described above, is the way you get your front and side stomach muscles involved with your strokes, giving you a lot more power and at the same time keeping your shoulders safe. You also need to use much more than just your arm and shoulder muscles when rolling a kayak. When you roll, keep your hands in front of your body (in the power position) and rotate at the waist to pull your paddle through the water. This will keep your shoulders safe, and give you the bracing support required to roll your kayak.

SHOULDER SAFETY

I've already touched on it in the section above, but shoulder safety is so important in that it deserves special emphasis. Shoulder dislocation is to kayaking what a blown knee is to skiing. Why is this injury so dreaded? The pain factor alone doesn't seem to drive the fear into paddlers' hearts; it's more the thought of having to go through surgery, of sitting idle through the prime spring and summer months, of the shoulder never again being as strong as it was. Unfortunately, these are substantiated concerns, and the truth of the matter is that if practiced improperly, rolling and bracing can be high-risk maneuvers for your shoulders. On that note, let's take a good look at how to keep your shoulders safe.

Having well-conditioned muscles around the shoulder will go a long way towards keeping the joint in place. Paddlers often have much stronger muscles on the back of their shoulders than the front, because the back of the shoulder muscles are used primarily in forward paddling. Because most shoulders dislocate forwards, your goal should be to make the front muscles equally as strong as the back. This is where back paddling practice comes in. If you're not entirely convinced of this weakness, then the next time you go paddling, I challenge you to take 25 hard

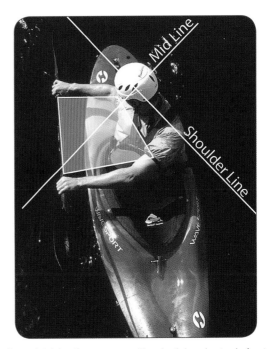

By maintaining the power position, both hands stay in front of the shoulder line and the arms, paddle and chest form a box.

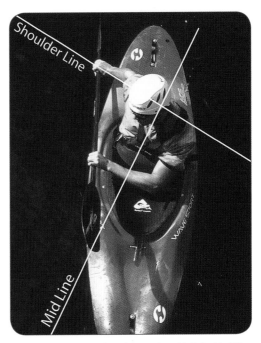

With poor torso rotation the rear hand falls behind the shoulder line and places the shoulder in a vulnerable position.

back strokes. I can guarantee that your shoulder muscles will burn in a way that they just don't when paddling forward, even over much greater distances.

Even with Superman's shoulders a dislocation can happen, so here are two simple rules that, when followed, will go a long way towards keeping your arms intact:

1. *Don't overextend your arms.* The idea of not overextending your arms is a simple concept to appreciate, but it isn't always so simple to apply. When you feel yourself flipping and or find yourself upside-down, the desire to keep your head above the water can easily override any safe paddling practices. Try to stay as relaxed as possible and fight the urge to use massive "Geronimo" braces.

2. *Maintain the power position!* (Also known as the Second Golden Rule.)

BRACING

My introduction to kayaking came from a week-long whitewater kayaking course on the Ottawa River. Of course, I was keen to learn the roll right away, but I remember my instructor, Perry MacGregor, telling me that the roll wasn't nearly as important for me to learn as the brace. In fact, with a good brace, he said that I wouldn't need to roll. I was 14 at the time, and so these words were a little lost on me. Rolling looked cool, and I wanted to do it. It took me a few days, but I learned to roll. I then proceeded to spend the next few days flipping and rolling my way down the rapids. But then, one day as I was starting to flip over, I instinctively reached out and slapped the water with my paddle in a brace position. If anyone had been watching, I'm sure they would have seen the lightbulb go on in my head. Rolling was cool, but bracing was even better! I also realized that rolling a kayak is nothing more than a dynamic brace performed from an inverted position. This is why it is so much better to learn good bracing technique before taking on the roll. It's a lot like learning to walk before you run.

There are two major forms of braces: the low and high brace. Both involve reaching out to the side of your kayak with your paddle and slapping the water with one blade, which provides the support needed for your body to right the boat. The only real difference between the two is the position of your paddle. It's critical to understand that the slap of the paddle just provides momentary support. Your body is responsible for the rest. Let's take a quick look at how to do it.

As you flip, the only way to right the kayak is by pulling up

1 The low brace uses the back side of your paddle against the water, which means rolling your paddle and hands below your elbows.

2 Slap the water at 90 degrees to get the most bracing power from your paddle.

with the knee that is going underwater. The only way to pull up with this bottom knee is to drop your head towards the water in the direction that you're flipping. This is completely counter-intuitive—and totally essential. Your head should be the last thing to come back up on a well-executed brace. If you lift your head up instead, you'll inadvertently pull on your top knee, which simply flips you even more quickly. To make sure that your head drops towards the water, try watching your slapping blade as you brace. It's harder to lift your head when you're looking down.

LOW BRACE

The low brace is so named because the paddle is kept very low. To set your paddle up for a low brace, sit upright and roll the paddle under your elbows so that your forearms are virtually vertical. Think of a pushup position. From here, you'll reach your paddle out at a 90 degree angle to your boat, so that one hand is at your belly button and the other is out over the water. You'll then smack the water with the non power-face or backside of your paddle blade. Practice slapping the water on alternating sides, making sure that your paddle hits the water flat. If your paddle has any type of feather, you'll need to rotate the paddle in

your grease hand to slap the water with a flat backside of your blade. After slapping the water, slide your paddle forward and inward, and roll your knuckles upward to clear the blade from the water.

When you get comfortable with the brace with your boat sitting flat on the water, start edging the boat slightly in the direction that you brace. As you slap the water, drop your head in that direction and pull up with your lower knee on that side to level off the kayak. Keep practicing these motions until they feel natural, and then start pushing your boat tilts further and further.

The low brace is a great reactionary brace that can be thrown in at a second's notice. Once you're comfortable with it, the low brace will become your best recovery technique, and it will also protect your shoulders really well from injury.

HIGH BRACE

The high brace is definitely the most powerful of the recovery techniques. A good paddler can even use the high brace to recover when their boat is almost completely upside-down! The problem with the high brace is that it's easy to rely on it too much, which can put your shoulders at risk. So the first

3 Drop your head toward the water. This action allows you to right your kayak completely with your lower body.

4 Roll your knuckles forward to clear the blade and finish in a forward position.

thing to keep in mind is that despite its name, you need to keep your paddle and your hands low and in front of your body. Otherwise, the high brace follows the same rules as the low brace—the main difference being that for the high brace you use your paddle in a "chin-up" position, instead of a "push up" position. This different position means that you'll use the power-face of your paddle blade instead of the backside to contact the water.

Starting with a flat boat, keep your elbows low and roll your paddle up until your forearms are almost vertical. You'll now reach out over the water at 90 degrees, with your inside arm low, in what is sometimes called the "nose pick" position. It's important to keep this hand low so that your paddle blade is as flat to the surface of the water as possible when it makes contact, because this will give you the most support. After slapping the water, slide your paddle inward, roll your knuckles backward and slice the blade out of the water.

Once you're comfortable high bracing on both sides, start tilting your boat slightly and combine the head drop and knee pull-up with your motions. This means that as you slap the water, you'll drop your head towards the water and pull up with your lower knee to right the kayak. Remember that looking at your active blade is a good habit to get into because it helps keep your head down.

As you perfect the high brace, you'll be amazed at powerful it can be. Just remember that for even the biggest high braces, you've got to keep your hands low to keep your shoulders safe from injury.

Low bracing while carving across a wave.

1 The high brace uses the power face of your paddle against the water, which means rolling your hands above your elbows.

2 Slap the water at 90 degrees to the kayak to get the most bracing power.

Drop your head towards the water as you level the boat with your lower body.

3 Drop your head towards the water as you level the boat with your lower body.

4 Roll your knuckles back and clear the blade in front of your body as you swing your body back over the top of the kayak.

Low bracing after seal launching into the water.

SCULLING

Sculling is a technique that lets you get steady support from your paddle blade by changing the angle at which it passes through the water. Learning to scull will go a long way towards helping you to roll a kayak because it will improve your paddle dexterity and allow you to get more and longer support from your paddle. Ultimately, you'll use your sculling technique to make small corrections and to compensate for things like waves and current that may be acting on your boat and paddle while rolling.

To simplify the development of your sculling technique, we'll start by looking at the sculling draw, which is the most effective means of moving your kayak laterally. This is a great way to begin because it uses very similar paddle motions to the sculling brace, but is easier to practice because your boat stays flat on the water.

SCULLING DRAW

The sculling draw is planted with your blade about two feet out to the side of your kayak, with the power face of your paddle blade facing your body. Make sure that the blade is completely immersed. For the most effective stroke, rotate your head and upper body aggressively to face your paddle and get your paddle shaft as vertical as possible. To get your paddle shaft vertical you'll need to reach across your upper body with your top hand. This takes some real balance, so you might want to start by practicing your draw stroke with your top hand lower, and in front of your face.

From this set-up position, the sculling draw involves moving your paddle blade along a short path forward and backward about a foot or two out to the side of your kayak, with a blade angle that opens your power face to the oncoming water and

1 Rotate your body to face your paddle while performing a sculling draw.

2 As you push your paddle towards the bow, keep your wrists cocked slightly back so that the power face catches water.

3 To change directions, curl your wrists forwards and pull the paddle back towards the stern.

4 Notice that the arms stay in a relatively fixed position. The forward and backward movement of your paddle should be driven by your torso rotation.

pulls your paddle away from your kayak. This blade angle is commonly referred to as a "climbing angle", which means that the leading edge of your paddle blade is higher than the trailing edge. It's the same as spreading jam on toast: picture the knife's angle as it glides over the bread's surface, leading edge higher than the trailing edge. To maintain a climbing angle on your blade while performing the sculling draw you'll cock your wrists back slightly as you slice your blade forward. You'll then make a quick transition and curl your wrists slightly forward as you slice your blade backward. Keep in mind that the change in blade angle is subtle. If you open your power face too much, you'll be pushing your kayak forward and backward rather than drawing it sideways.

Using this sculling technique, you can apply steady drawing pressure with your paddle blade and move your boat laterally at a surprising speed. Don't forget that just like any other stroke, the power for your sculling draw comes from your torso rotation. This is why it's so important that you turn your body aggressively into the stroke. The forward and backward movement of your paddle can then be driven by your torso rotation, while your arms will stay in a relatively fixed position.

SCULLING BRACE

The sculling brace is an advanced bracing technique that lets you get steady support from your paddle blade. It incorporates a combination of the sculling draw technique and your high brace technique.

Like the sculling draw, the key to getting steady support for your sculling brace is to keep your paddle moving back and forth, parallel to your kayak, with a climbing angle on your blade. The combination of your paddle's movement along with its climbing angle will keep your paddle blade near the surface of the water, while providing you with steady support.

Start practicing the sculling brace with your boat flat on the water and your paddle in the high brace position. Since the goal is to apply steady downward pressure from your sculling brace, you'll want to keep your hands low (under your chin) and your paddle as horizontal as you comfortably can. Keeping

Start practicing the sculling brace with your boat flat on the water and your paddle in the high brace position.

your hands in this low, high brace position also keeps your shoulders safe. From this position, sweep your paddle forward and backward across the surface of the water about two feet out to the side of your kayak. Focus on keeping a climbing angle on your blade, using your torso rotation to move the paddle back and forth, and making quick transitions from one climbing angle to the next.

As you become more comfortable and confident with these motions, you can start edging your kayak and letting your weight fall over to the side so that your paddle needs to supply actual bracing support. You'll find that your paddle motions need to become more aggressive as you put weight on it and start relying on it for real bracing power. Of course, the more you do so, the more important it becomes that you keep your hands low to keep your shoulders safe.

1 *The sculling brace is a powerful stroke, so it is critical that you keep your hands low to keep your shoulders safe.*

2 *As you sweep your paddle towards the stern, your wrists should be curled slightly forward to keep a climbing angle on your blade.*

3 *As you sweep your paddle towards the bow, cock your wrists slightly back to keep the climbing angle on your blade.*

4 *To provide the power to support your body, the sculling brace needs to be quick and aggressive.*

HIP SNAP

The hip snap (or hip flick) refers to the action of rotating your hips to right your kayak. The hip snap is without a doubt the single most important technique to master in order to have success with your braces and your roll.

The idea behind the hip snap is simple. By staying loose at your waist (applying the First Golden Rule by separating your upper and lower body movements), you can use your knee to roll your hips and your kayak upright while your body remains in the water. To do this effectively, you'll need some form of support for your upper body. For most rolls, your paddle provides this support. For a hand roll, your hands provide the support. The fact that your hands can provide enough support against the water to roll your kayak is a testament to how important the hip snap is for the roll.

HIP SNAP PRACTICE

As I just mentioned, the key to an effective hip snap is applying the First Golden Rule, which means staying loose at the waist and letting your upper and lower body work independently and co-operatively with each other. A great test of your ability to do this can be done while sitting still in your kayak on flat water. While holding your paddle horizontally in front of your body and keeping your upper body as still as possible, use your hips and knees to rock your kayak from one edge to another. Imagine that your paddle is a serving tray with your favorite cocktail on it. You'll need to keep your upper body and your paddle as still as possible so that you don't spill a drop while your lower body rocks your boat back and forth. This avoids the full body wag, and truly tests your ability to let the lower and upper parts of your body work separately in co-operation.

The next drill involves holding onto something that is stable enough to keep your head above the water when your kayak is completely overturned. It can be done alone or with the help of a friend. Alone, you can use the side of a pool or a low dock. With a friend, you can use an end of his or her kayak. With a firm grip on your support, you'll lean right over on your side

and lay your cheek on your hands. Relax your hips as much as possible and pull your top knee over so that the kayak collapses on top of you. You'll know that your hips are loose enough and that your kayak has flipped over all the way when you feel its cockpit rim come into contact with your side.

It's now time to roll the boat upright using your hip snap. Keeping your cheek on your hands, pull the trailing knee (the one that's underwater) up toward your body and roll your hips and kayak as upright as possible. When you feel the lower cockpit rim come into contact with your side, you'll know that you've rotated the kayak as far as possible. For this drill, maintain your grip on whatever is supporting you, keep your cheek on your hands, and use your knees and hips to roll the kayak upside-down again so that you can repeat these steps.

The goal is to maximize your hip rotation while exerting the least amount of pressure on your hands. By using the bow of a friend's kayak, you'll be able gauge how much you are pushing down with your hands. If you are pushing down too aggressively, the bow of their kayak will be forced underwater. Ideally, you should be able to keep the deck of your friend's kayak dry when you perform this drill.

When you get comfortable with your hip snap on one side,

Lie your head on the bow of a friend's kayak and use your knees to pull the kayak completely upside-down. Keeping your head down, roll your boat upright using the lower knee while pushing as little as possible on your friend's kayak.

Raising your head will cause you to push down on the bow of your friend's kayak and makes rolling the kayak upright much more difficult. You should be able to keep their bow dry.

practice it on the other. Having an effective hip snap on both sides will come in handy for kayak rescues, and it will provide you with an even better understanding of the technique.

T-RESCUE

For a T-rescue, the rescuer offers one end of his or her kayak to an upside-down paddler, which the upside-down paddler can then use to hip snap their boat upright. The T-rescue is the most basic form of kayak rescue and is really only used between instructors and students; it's unreasonable for a kayaker to expect a T-rescue when out on the river. Still, the T-rescue is a great practice when you're learning to roll. It will help you to relax and orient yourself when you're upside-down underwater, and it will force you to use your hip snap from a completely inverted position.

With a rescuer close by and ready, you'll flip yourself upside-down and tuck your body forward against the deck of your kayak. If you're not wearing nose plugs this will result in a major sinus flushing, but it's important that you tuck forward because it protects your face and body, and it puts you in a position that is similar to that which you'll use when rolling. Reach up to the

surface with both hands, one on each side of your kayak, and slap the bottom of your boat three times to let the rescuer know you're ready for his or her help.

While waiting for the rescuer, your job is now to provide them with as large a target area a possible: do this by running your arms alongside your kayak hull. The rescuer will approach your overturned kayak at 90 degrees and gently run their bow into the side of your kayak in the area that your arms are sweeping. If they're on target, one of your arms will soon bump into the bow of the rescuer's kayak. Grab the rescuer's kayak with both hands.

The success of the T-rescue now depends on your ability to hip snap your kayak upright. With a firm grip on the bow of the rescue boat, gently draw your head and body towards the surface out at 90 degrees to your kayak. The idea isn't to use your arms to pull your head and body out of the water; you're simply trying to get your body as close to the water's surface as possible. From this position, you should be able to right your kayak with your hip snap, while placing a minimum amount of pressure on the bow of the rescue boat. If you're straining to right your kayak, or if the bow of the rescue boat is being pushed underwater, you'll know that you're pushing too aggressively with your arms.

A T-rescue is great practice when you're learning to roll. It forces you to orient yourself underwater and to use your hip snap from a completely inverted position.

CHAPTER 3

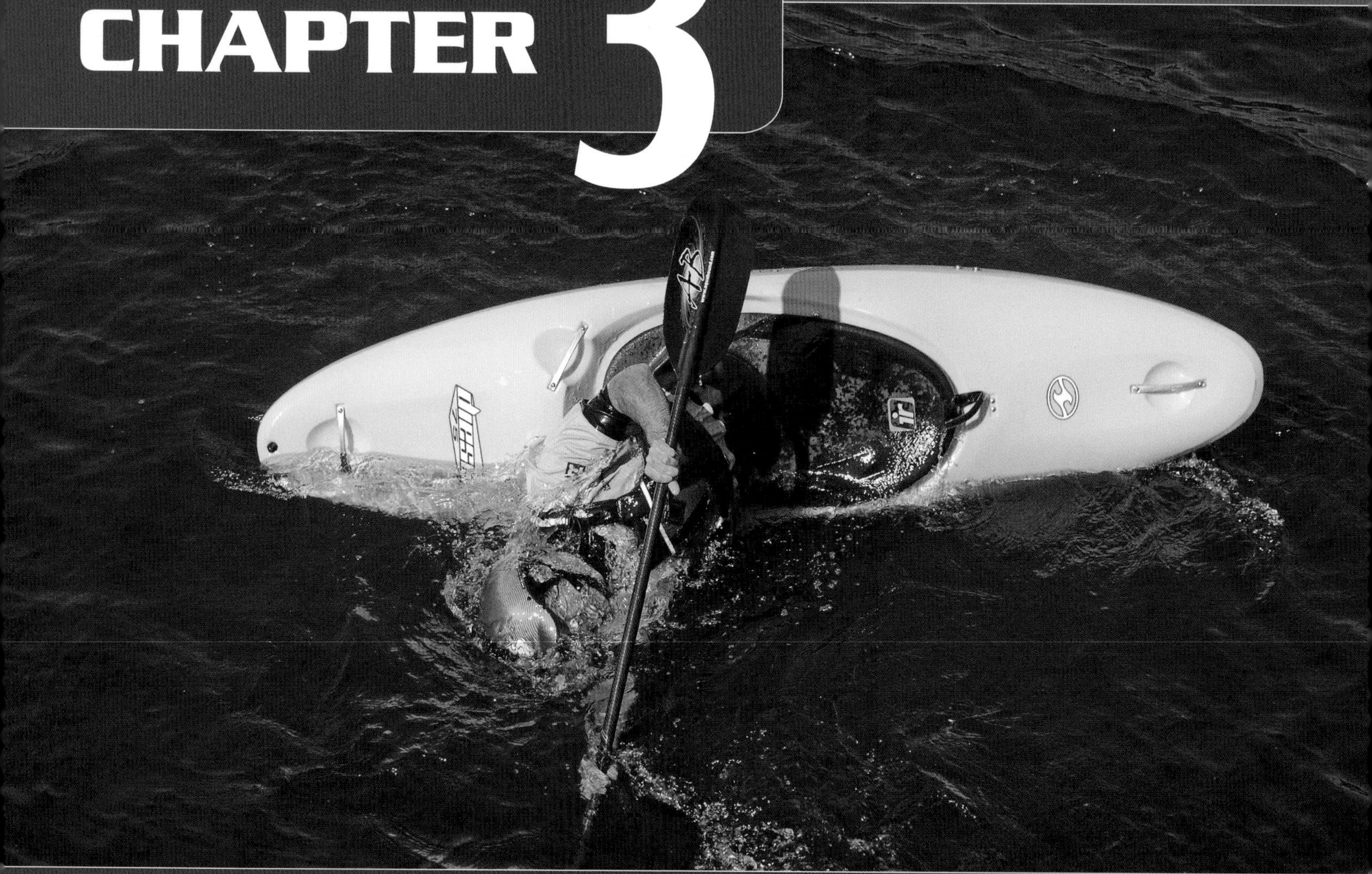

ROLLING A KAYAK

You might find this hard to believe, but there are over 100 different types of rolls being put to practice today. The vast majority of these rolls were developed by Inuit kayak hunters, who relied on them for survival in freezing arctic waters. In particular, an enormous amount of knowledge has come from the kayakers of Greenland whose paddling style is still practiced and greatly respected by many sea kayakers today. Rather than taking a cursory look at a broad range of specialized rolling techniques, we're going to focus our attention on the details of the most common types of rolls.

In this chapter, we're going to look at the two most basic rolling methods: the C-to-C and sweep rolls. Both of these rolls represent a great starting ground when learning, although there is a great debate among kayak instructors as to which technique is the best to teach new kayakers. In my opinion, there is no correct answer to this question. I've taught both techniques extensively and have found that different people take to different techniques more quickly—it's almost completely arbitrary. In some cases, I've even started out teaching one type of roll and after watching a kayaker struggle with it, have switched techniques with great success. After looking at these two rolls, we'll take a look at some of the common problems people have with them, along with their solutions.

The idea behind these rolls (and all other rolls for that matter) is quite simple. To roll a kayak upright from the upside-down position, you're going to extend your body out to the side and get yourself as close to the surface of the water as possible. From this position, your paddle will act like a brace and provide the support needed to hip snap your kayak upright. When practicing your hip snap (which we looked at earlier), the support needed to do it came from a friend's kayak, or from the side of a pool or dock. In the description of the hip snap drills, I stressed the need to maximize the hip movement while exerting the least amount of pressure on your hands. This is all the more important when attempting an unassisted roll—you'll get far less purchase from your paddle than you did from the kayak or the pool side.

As your hips roll your kayak upright and under your body, your head, upper body, and lower body work together to finish the roll. This is where the bracing technique we looked at earlier comes in, and where I'll again emphasize the importance of dropping your head towards the water. By dropping your head to the water, you allow your bottom knee to continue to pull your kayak upright. At the same time, dropping your head keeps your centre of gravity low while your body moves over your kayak. If you lift your head instead, you'll pull on your top knee, which will effectively pull your kayak back upside-down.

Again I'll acknowledge that dropping your head towards the water is extremely counter-intuitive—but I'll also restate that it's absolutely essential! Your head should be the last part of your body to come back up.

THE C-TO-C AND SWEEP ROLLS

The C-to-C and sweep rolls are the two most popular rolls for new paddlers to learn and the most common rolls that you'll see being used in real life. What makes them so popular is the fact that they break the roll into a series of three defined, easy-to-understand steps. As I already mentioned, there is an ongoing debate about which roll is best to learn first and which I'm not really going to get into. What I will tell you is that a sweep roll is usually more effective, and although you may prefer to learn the C-to-C roll first, over time your roll may evolve into a sweeping style. Because the sweep roll requires less set-up, the paddle doesn't usually end up as deep in the water, giving you a longer-lasting support (brace) from your paddle. This means that the hip snap can be more fluid and less abrupt. The sweep roll can be slightly more difficult to learn, however, because two steps from the C-to-C roll are combined into a single motion, which opens up a bit more room for error.

Whatever you learn, your "natural roll" will just be the one you feel most comfortable with and typically use the most often. It is normal for your "natural roll" to be redefined over time as you develop other skills and preferences.

I'm now going to break down the C-to-C and sweep rolls into three distinct steps, while at the same time looking at the differences between the two rolls. The three distinct steps are the set-up, the catch, and the recovery.

THE SET-UP

The C-to-C and sweep rolls both start from the same set-up position. As soon as you've flipped over, your first order of business is to get into this position. When learning, you're best to get into the set-up position before flipping over—it can be disorienting to be upside-down the first few times. With practice, you'll be able to assume this set-up position underwater, without having to think about it.

To get in the set-up position, place your paddle alongside your kayak with the forward blade flat to the water's surface and the power face up. Which side of the kayak you set up on is generally determined by your control hand side. (The control hand is the one that stays glued to your paddle.) Most people prefer to set the paddle up with their control hand closest to the bow. Because most paddlers have a right-side control hand, the paddle is most often placed on the left side of the kayak with the right hand closest to the bow.

Tuck your head and body forward and rotate your upper body towards your paddle as you push the paddle right into the water, keeping it flat and parallel to the boat. Remember to use torso rotation (the Third Golden Rule), and maintain your power position (the Second Golden Rule) to keep your hands in front of your upper body. Applying this to your set-up position means that you'll turn your chest to face towards the shaft of your paddle.

There are a couple of good reasons for starting with this set-up position. Tucking forward provides you with the most protection while under water, keeping your helmet and life jacket between you and any looming rocks. Also, because being

The ideal set-up position involves placing your paddle alongside the kayak with the forward blade flat to the water's surface and your head and body turned towards your paddle.

When setting up underwater, the further out to the side you can get your body, the more easily your hip snap will be able to right your kayak.

LEARNING TIP

As an instructor, I confess that one of the most humorous things to watch is when a paddler who is learning to roll sets up and throws themselves upside-down, only to get stuck with their boat on edge and their head underwater. This awkward position usually results when a paddler flips over with their body in an upright position. By doing so, the paddler's lifejacket acts as a brace on the flipping side of the kayak. If you are encountering this problem, tuck further forward in your set-up position when flipping upside-down, and know that this is a problem common to beginners that doesn't tend to last long. If you do get stuck on edge, you may need to wiggle your hips and take an underwater stroke to pull your boat completely upside-down.

upside-down can be very disorienting, the set-up position gives you a consistent starting point from which you can always get your bearings.

There are a couple of cues to be aware of when setting up under water. Your forearms should press against the side of your kayak and your hands should be in the air. You should also be extending your body out to the side so that your head is as close to the surface as possible. The further out to the side you can get your body, the more easily your hip snap will be able to right your kayak. This is the most awkward part of the roll, because it requires some aggressive stretching and twisting. If you can feel the cockpit rim of your kayak digging into your side, you know that you're stretching out to the side as far as possible and in a good position to start your roll.

1 The C-to-C roll involves pivoting the paddle out to 90 degrees.

2 With your paddle blade out at 90degrees and as close to the surface of the water as possible, pull downwards to "catch" water and hip snap.

THE CATCH

The catch refers to the part of the roll where you grab water with your blade to support your upper body while you hip snap your kayak upright. The catch is also where the sweep and C-to-C rolls start to differ.

I must emphasize that the catch is not about grabbing water to pull yourself upright. Your paddle just won't supply enough support to do this, and trying to do so will put an undue amount of stress on your body. Remember how, when practicing the hip snap, you had to minimize the use of your arms. If you were successful in doing this, then you have felt how little pressure is needed from your paddle to roll the boat upright with your trailing knee (the knee that will be last out of the water when you roll upright).

You will get the most support or leverage from your blade when it's out at 90 degrees (perpendicular) to your kayak.

THE C-TO-C ROLL CATCH

Swing the paddle blade on your control hand side so it is at an angle of 90 degrees to the side of your kayak. Use your other forearm as a pivot against the kayak to keeps the other blade over the bottom of your upside-down boat.

Maintain your power position at all times. This means that as you swing your control arm paddle blade out to 90 degrees, twist your upper body to keep your hands in front of your body.

With your paddle blade out at 90 degrees and as close to the surface of the water as possible, pull downwards on your paddle and "catch" the water. When you feel the catch, perform a strong hip snap.

LEARNING TIP

For either the sweep or C-to-C roll, one of the best ways to make sure that you maintain the power position and rotate your torso during your roll is to watch your active blade as it moves. If you don't like to open your eyes underwater, then just imagine that you're watching the blade, or better yet, use a diving mask or goggles when you're learning. Turning your head in time with your active blade will naturally turn your upper body at the same rate, and help keep your shoulders safe. Watching your active blade will also keep your center of gravity low and make rolling easier.

① *The sweep roll involves catching water with the power face of your paddle with a sculling angle on it as you sweep out to 90-degrees.*

② *As your paddle gets closer to 90 degrees (it's most powerful position to catch water), the more aggressively you'll be able to apply downward pressure on your paddle and snap your hips.*

THE SWEEP ROLL CATCH

Your paddle goes through very similar motions for the sweep roll. The difference is that you start applying downward pressure on the blade sooner, and so have a longer period of leverage from your blade.

Swing the paddle blade on your control hand side so it is at an angle of 90 degrees to the side of your kayak, but do it in a wider arc than you did for the C-to-C. This will maximize leverage on your blade. This also means that the forearm will not remain against your kayak as a pivot. Instead, keep your other arm bent, close to your body, and relatively passive as it sweeps out from your kayak.

As with the C-to-C roll, you absolutely must maintain your power position at all times. Your arms should actually stay in a relatively fixed position while your torso rotation drives the sweeping motion of your paddle.

Keep your blade near the surface of the water while you sweep and pull downwards on it. This will be one of your biggest challenges and the only way to do it effectively is to maintain a slight climbing angle on the paddle blade. This means keeping the leading edge of the blade slightly higher so that it wants to "climb" to the surface. You don't need very much climbing angle on your paddle, because you won't be applying too much downward pressure on it, right? It's also important to understand that your paddle won't provide as much support at the beginning of its travels (just as a brace planted at the bow of your kayak wouldn't give you much bracing power), so don't try to snap your hips too aggressively too early.

Without having started the hip snap yet, you'll find that even the initial pressure you apply on your paddle will draw your head and body slightly closer to the surface, and start your kayak's rolling motion. This action alone can roll your kayak a good twenty degrees up before you even start your hip snap. As your paddle sweeps further out, you'll gain more and more leverage, and you can begin snapping your hips to right the boat. Because this sweep gives you an extended period of time with support, you can snap your hips in a smoother, slightly less "jerky" motion than is required for the C-to-C roll.

THE RECOVERY

The recovery is the final stage of your roll and is how your body ends up in its position atop your kayak. If you have set up properly, used a powerful hip snap, and maintained the power position throughout, then the recovery is relatively straightforward.

One of the most common problems during the recovery phase is a premature lifting of the head, which causes you to pull

Watching the active blade throughout the roll ensures that your head is the last part of your body to return to its position over your kayak.

up on your top knee and yank your kayak back upside-down. Your head should be the last part of your body to return to its position over the kayak. Watching your active blade throughout should reduce or eliminate this problem.

There is some debate about the recovery path your body should take after the catch and the hip snap. Most people find that it helps to lean slightly backward during the final stages of the roll because it lowers one's center of gravity. Others believe that the roll should be finished with your body swinging forward over the bow of your kayak to help protect your face from rocks. I am strongly against swinging the body forward because it raises your center of gravity and hinders your hip snap, making the roll more difficult and less reliable. This means there's a better chance of blowing your roll and going back underwater. Furthermore, it's questionable that swinging your body forward provides additional protection to your face, because when executed properly, your head should stay close to the surface and well-hidden behind your arms and paddle throughout the roll. It is the awkward transition into the set-up position immediately after flipping upside-down that puts your face in the most vulnerable position—and that neither of these rolls can avoid. (In this regard, the back deck roll has a distinct advantage, and is why I use it 99% of the time... but that's

another story. For more information about the back deck roll, see Chapter 4, "Other Types of Rolls".)

If all goes well during the recovery stage of your roll, you should finish over top your kayak with a slight backward lean, your head and torso turned to face your active blade. Your wrists should be cocked back so that your blade is on a climbing angle as you turn your body back to your normal sitting position, and push your paddle blade towards your toes.

WHITEWATER TIP

For whitewater kayakers, evolutions in boat design are making the sweep roll the more popular roll to learn. Whitewater kayaks have become wider, deeper and boxier in cross-sectional shape. These features don't allow a paddler to reach as close to the surface with head, body and paddle during the set-up. During the C-to-C roll, when you have to swing your paddle out to 90 degrees, the shape of these newer boats can make it very difficult to keep the active blade near the surface and swing the other blade over the hull of the kayak. This challenge is accentuated for paddlers with shorter torsos and/or arms.

A COMPARISON OF THE C-TO-C AND SWEEP ROLLS

C-TO-C ROLL

1 Start the C-to-C roll from the regular set-up position.

2 With the left arm acting as a pivot against the kayak, sweep the right blade out to 90 degrees.

SWEEP ROLL

1 Start from the regular set-up position and begin sweeping your paddle out to 90 degrees.

2 With a slight climbing angle on the blade, apply downward pressure duing the sweeping motion and the boat will already begin to roll upright.

③ Pull down on the paddle to provide the momentary leverage needed to hip snap the boat upright.

④ Watch the active blade so that your head is the last thing to come out of the water, and to help keep your shoulders safe.

③ Let your head follow the active blade during the sweep and hip snap to roll the boat upright.

④ Watch the active blade so that your head is the last thing to come out of the water, and to help keep your shoulders safe.

THE EXTENDED PADDLE ROLL (PAWLATA)

If you're having trouble getting yourself upright with the C-to-C or sweep rolls, you might want to try the extended paddle roll, otherwise known as the "Pawlata". The Pawlata roll can be done just like the C-to-C or sweep roll, the only difference being that you move your hands to one end of your paddle, allowing your active blade to reach further out from your kayak. This extension allows your paddle to achieve considerably more bracing power, which gives the other elements of your roll a little more room for error. Many instructors teach the Pawlata roll to new paddlers first, with great success.

To set up for an extended paddle roll, assume your regular set-up position, (before flipping or while underwater), and slide your hands down the paddle shaft until you're grasping the back blade with your back pivot hand, and holding the paddle shaft comfortably with your control hand. With your paddle held in this extended position, perform a C-to-C or sweep roll. If you're using the sweep roll technique with an extended paddle, be careful not to rush the hip snap, because it will take longer for your blade to sweep out to 90 degrees from your kayak.

① *The set-up for the extended paddle roll is the same as the standard roll, only your hands are moved to one end of the paddle.*

② *It will take longer to sweep your paddle out to 90 degrees, so don't rush your hip snap.*

③ *Although your paddle will provide much more leverage when held in the extended position, a strong hip snap should be your focus.*

④ *Watching the active blade helps keep your head down throughout the roll and ensures a safe recovery position.*

COMMON PROBLEMS AND SOLUTIONS

As an instructor, the kayak roll is one of the most challenging skills to teach, but it's also one of the most enjoyable, entertaining, and rewarding techniques to pass on. For the developing kayaker, learning to roll can be tricky, but for most people, nailing the first roll is one of the most exciting and confidence-building moments that kayaking can offer.

Of course, the challenges that make the roll so rewarding can also make it one of the most frustrating techniques to learn. There are many different things that can go wrong, and often one mistake will set off a chain reaction of other errors. The biggest challenge for instructors is to recognize what mistakes are being made, follow them back, and identify the roots of problems. As the learning paddler, this process is almost impossible to do for yourself, and the reason that professional instruction is so valuable. Because of this, I will explain problems and solutions from the perspective of an instructor, but for those paddlers learning to roll who are reading this, this segment should provide some clarity about the most common issues that will prevent your roll from succeeding.

I will go over these most common problems chronologically, from those that happen in the earliest stages, to those that happen in the later stages of the roll. This means that issues will be discussed in the order that they would need to be dealt with in a learning situation.

SETTING UP UNDER THE KAYAK

One of the first and most common problems you'll encounter is a paddler who sets up with their body tucked forward, instead of leaning out to the side of their kayak and getting their face and body as close to the surface as they can. This will dramatically impede their ability to keep their blade near the surface as they sweep it out to 90 degrees for either the sweep or C-to-C roll. But even worse, by setting up under the kayak instead of to the side, the paddler will only be able to use a portion of their hip snap. Their hip snap will be spent before their kayak has been rolled upright, and leave them with no option but to aggressively attempt to finish the roll by throwing their head and body upward (which rarely works).

SOLUTION

To teach a paddler to lean as far as possible out to the side as possible, stand in waist-deep water on the side of their kayak that their paddle will end up on when they're upside-down. Let

Setting up with your body tucked forward under the kayak will impede your ability to keep your blade near the surface as you sweep it out to 90 degrees, and it will dramatically hinder your hip snap.

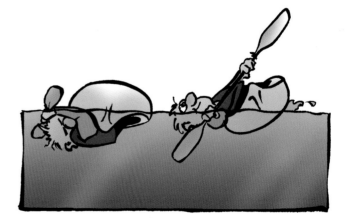

Setting up with your body aggressively leaning out to the side of the kayak allows you to use your hip snap to its full capacity and allows your paddle to stay closest to the surface.

them know that their job is to get the paddle to the surface in the set-up position. When they are upside-down and set up, lightly grab the shaft of the paddle and pull upward. This will pull their body out to the side of the kayak. By pulling their body slowly into position and holding it there for them, you'll help imprint how the position should feel when they do it on their own.

What you do from this point depends on what stage the paddler is at with their roll, and should be prearranged with the paddler before they flip. For beginners, you might gently support the blade and guide the paddle through its sweeping motions while the paddler focuses their attention on their hip snap. For more advanced rollers, you might want them to do the rest of the roll on their own. If this is the case, prearrange with them to wait for your slap on the hull of their kayak, so you can step clear and avoid getting speared by their paddle blade.

1 The underwater forward stroke is usually a result of a paddler relying too heavily on their paddle for support.

LEARNING TIP

Reduced flexibility and the subsequent inability to get the body close to the surface is one of the main reasons why overweight paddlers often have more trouble rolling. Their girth prevents their head and body from extending as far out to the side of the kayak and so their paddle must provide more bracing support. For this reason, the sweep roll is usually the best rolling technique for overweight paddlers to learn because the paddle provides more and longer support. The first part of the sweep will also serve to pull their head and body closer to the surface so that the hip snap can complete the roll more effectively.

UNDERWATER FORWARD STROKE

The underwater forward stroke is a phenomenon common to paddlers who rely too heavily on their paddle for support and who pull downward on their paddle from its set-up position, instead of sweeping the blade outward across the water surface. The result is that instead of drawing the head and body closer

2 Instead of the paddle sweeping out to 90 degrees across the water, the paddle is pulled directly downward from the set-up position.

If the active blade doesn't have a slight climbing angle, the paddle will dive during the sweep roll, making for a tough recovery.

to the surface of the water, the paddle will actually draw the head and body deeper underwater and make it impossible for the hip snap to fully right the kayak. For this reason, the underwater forward stroke is usually followed by a desperate toss of the head and body into the air, which seldom results in a successful roll.

SOLUTION

The best way to help a paddler who is taking underwater forward strokes instead of sweeping their paddle out across the surface of the water is to get into waist deep water with them and help guide their paddle through the sweeping motion. They will likely be very surprised by how far out to the side of their kayak they are required to stretch, and just feeling it under your guidance may show them the light. For the first few times, get them to focus on their hip snap and on minimizing the amount of pressure they place on their paddle. Next, let them know that

you're going to move their paddle slowly and that you want them to really think about how far out to the side they are being stretched. At this point, they should no longer be taking the underwater forward stroke. However, if they're doing a sweep roll, they could now be dealing with a diving paddle.

PADDLE DIVES WHEN SWEEPING

During the sweep roll, the active blade must have a slight climbing angle so that it continuously works its way toward the surface while the paddler sweeps it out to 90 degrees and applies downward pressure. Without this slight climbing angle, the blade will dive underwater through the sweeping motion. This results in the same problem that is experienced by those suffering from the underwater forward stroke. Instead of drawing the head and body closer to the surface of the water, the sweeping motions will actually draw the head and body deeper underwater and make it impossible for the hip snap to fully right the kayak. It is because of this problem that many instructors will teach the C-to-C roll first. Learning paddlers often won't have the paddle dexterity or awareness to differentiate between a diving and climbing blade angle, especially when faced with the initial disorientation of being upside-down.

SOLUTION

If a paddler is repeatedly slicing their paddle downward during the sweeping phase of their roll, there are a number of possible solutions. If the paddler hasn't yet learned and practiced the sculling draw or the sculling brace, going over these can be extremely useful. It will teach them the correct body movement and the feel of support that one gets from a paddle when a climbing angle is used successfully. This is also a great time to emphasize the need for a relaxed grip on the paddle.

You might also want to stand in the water with the paddler and help guide their paddle through the sweeping motion on the correct angle. Doing this a few times will often be enough for a paddler to learn and to mimic the motions. If you notice that they have a white-knuckled grip on their paddle, get them to ease up on it. A relaxed (but not loose) grip will let them get a better feel for how the paddle is acting in the water.

Another simple correction that you can try is to have the paddler set-up and sweep with their wrists cocked slightly inward.

HEAD LIFT

Prematurely lifting the head is a very common problem and is often a symptom of one of the problems discussed above. Sometimes though, a paddler will set up and execute their role to perfection, only to blow it by lifting their head out of the water too early. It's a very common error because all natural

Prematurely lifting the head is the most common rolling problem and rarely ends with success.

instincts are telling the paddler to get their head out of the water. It's also common because it is one of the last steps to the roll, and paddlers will often focus so much attention on the movement of their paddle that their hip snap is forgotten. As a result, the head and body are thrown skywards in a last-ditch attempt to right the kayak.

SOLUTION

The simple solution to stopping an early head lift is to have the paddler watch their active blade throughout the roll. By keeping their eyes on that blade, it will be impossible for them to lift their head. This is where a diving mask and goggles come in handy.

If this doesn't immediately solve the problem, the issue can likely be traced back to their hip snap. They might lack confidence in their hip snap, or they might be so focused on the movement of their paddle that the hip snap gets neglected. The easiest way to fix this problem is often to take a few steps

back and simplify the roll. Start by standing in the water with the paddler and guide their paddle through its movement, asking the paddler to focus their attention on making a full and complete hip snap while placing a minimal amount of pressure on their paddle. Once the hip snap is smooth and complete, you can start to let them take more control of their paddle, although you can still hold and offer some support to the active blade. It may take a few sessions, but eventually the hip snap and the paddle motions will become more natural and coordinated.

PIVOT ARM PUNCH

The pivot arm punch is an easily identifiable problem because the paddler will finish their rolling motions (usually unsuccessfully) with their pivot arm high in the air and their active blade deep in the water. By pushing their pivot arm into the air, the paddle is forced into a more vertical position and the pressure applied on the active blade becomes a lateral force, (more like a draw

When teaching the roll, you can support the kayakers body with your chest so that your hands are free to manipulate their paddle, while their head stays out of the water so that they can hear your instructions.

1 *The paddler begins in a good position.*

2 *The paddler punches their pivot arm instead of keeping it in a relatively low fixed position, and the active blade dives.*

3 *The active blade dives as the paddler attempts to right their boat with the hip snap.*

4 *The roll fails.*

stroke), rather than a downward, bracing force. The pivot arm must stay in a relatively fixed low position throughout the roll to keep the paddle as horizontal as possible.

SOLUTION

The key to avoiding a pivot arm punch is to keep the pivot arm bent and close to the body and to keep the pivot arm hand in front of the chest. For both the C-to-C and sweep rolls, the pivot arm must not straighten or reach above eye level. When dealing with a paddler who is doing a pivot arm punch, ask them to keep their pivot arm elbow against their side and that hand in front of their chest. If this doesn't solve the problem, you'll probably need to stand in the water and walk them through the steps. Since it will be helpful to be able to talk them as you do so, you'll want to hold their head above the water. The best way to do this is to stand on the rolling side of their kayak, just behind their body while they are still upright. Have them assume their set-up position and slowly fall towards the water in your direction while you support them, either under their arm or by grabbing hold of their PFD. Another option is to stand directly beside the kayak and support their body with your chest. Either way, they can now completely right their kayak while you keep their head above water. You can now talk them through the paddle movement and even use one of your hands to help guide them. Support the paddler instead of the paddle during this drill, because you want to avoid forcing them to put pressure on their blade.

TEACHING THE ROLL

Teaching the kayak roll is an exercise in patience and communication. For many instructors, it is the most enjoyable kayak skill to teach for the challenges involved, and for the feeling of satisfaction that comes from successfully helping a paddler learn to roll.

Before looking at some of the ways to teach the roll, it's important that I preface this section by making it clear that the techniques presented here come from my years spent teaching the roll, and working and learning from other instructors. Although they are time-tested and proven methods, they certainly don't represent the only way to teach the kayak roll.

One of the most important things to do as an instructor is to keep in perspective how difficult and emotionally taxing things—which may seem simple to an experienced paddler—can be for new paddlers. Fear and frustration can be powerful hindrances to learning. For these reasons, it should be a priority to develop and support the beginner paddler's comfort in being upside-down underwater—before they have an opportunity to flip unexpectedly and scare themselves—and it is why I recommend starting with the wet exit.

Every paddler has a different comfort level on the water. Some paddlers won't mind flipping and swimming on their own accord. For others, flipping upside-down will be a terrifying experience, even with you standing right beside them in the water. For more anxious paddlers, try the following progression. Start by standing in waist-deep water with the paddler facing you in their kayak. Ask the paddler to hug their deck while you flip them over and then immediately flip them back upright. As they gain confidence, you can ask them to slap the hull of their kayak when they want to be rolled up so they can safely experiment with being upside-down a little longer. It won't be long before they will have the confidence to try the wet exit with you holding onto their kayak, ready to roll them upright in case they suddenly feel like they "can't get out". After a few wet exits with you on hand, they'll be ready to flip over themselves and perform the wet exit with your more distant supervision.

Once a paddler is comfortable with the idea of being underwater, you can start teaching the hip snap, discussed in Chapter 2, "Fundamentals". Ask the paddler to first practice rocking their boat back and forth while keeping their upper body still and upright. This teaches them to stay loose at the hips, which allows their upper and lower bodies to work separately and cooperatively with each other. Next, ask the paddler to practice their hip snap while on their side and holding something stable, such as the side of a pool, a low dock, or the bow of a friend's boat. Once they have developed a full hip snap and learned to keep the head down throughout, try a few T-

rescues. When a T-rescue can be performed competently on both sides, a paddler is ready to learn to roll.

As with teaching any skill, remember that different people learn in different ways, and no one way is better than another. On one end of the spectrum you have people who learn visually and through action. No matter how effectively you break down the technique verbally, this type of person really needs to see it and/or attempt it to fully understand it. On the other end of the spectrum you have people who learn in a very technical fashion and who need to be given clear verbal breakdown of the method with obvious landmarks. Most people fall somewhere in between these two ends and will need the roll to be both demonstrated and broken down in a clear and simple manner. This is not only important when introducing the roll, but it is equally important when working with a paddler one-on-one, while standing in the water. As clearly as you may be verbally communicating what you would like them to do, you may have to hop into your kayak and demonstrate it.

With regards to which roll is the best to teach a learning paddler, there is no correct answer. As I mentioned earlier, some instructors will very successfully teach the Pawlata roll first. The Pawlata is much more common among sea kayakers and much less so among whitewater kayakers because the latter need to be ready to go immediately after rolling up, making it preferable to not move the hands around on the paddle. I prefer to teach a standard C-to-C or sweep roll because it promotes good rolling technique from the very beginning and it helps to develop paddle dexterity.

Whichever roll you decide to teach, don't give the paddler any options early on. The simpler you can keep it, the better

chance they have at rolling successfully. If after working on a particular type of roll for a while, you decide that it would be best to try a different style, no problem. In the interests of being attentive and flexible, feel free to adapt your teaching technique as necessary, but understand that you want to limit how often you switch techniques.

I have always found the most successful teaching progression starts with me standing in the water with the paddler. I ask them to focus on setting up with their paddle high out of the water, and their head and body leaning far out to the side. I ask them beforehand to let me guide their paddle, while they focus their attention on making a complete and powerful hip snap and keeping their head down. By repeating these motions, the paddler learns how their paddle should move through its set-up and catch phase. Once they are setting their paddle up

One of the best ways to build the confidence of beginning paddlers who are anxious about flipping is to roll their kayak for them until they become comfortable with the feeling of being upside-down.

nice and high out of the water, hip snapping effectively, and keeping their head down throughout the roll, they are ready to start taking more control of their own paddle. At this point I stand right behind their body while they are still upright. While supporting them either under their arm or by grabbing hold of their PFD, I have them slowly fall towards me. They can now completely right their kayak while I keep their head just above water. If required, I talk them through the paddle motion and even use one of my hands to help guide them. The key, as mentioned earlier, is to support the paddler not the blade, so that they do not have to put too much pressure on their paddle.

These assisted rolling practice drills will develop good technique over time. Some paddlers will catch on right away, while other paddlers may need a number of sessions before it clicks. Just stay patient, attentive, flexible, and positive. Another thing to keep in mind is that rolling uses muscles in ways that a learning paddler isn't used to. This fact, combined with the mental challenges of picking up a new skill, mean that there is a point at which "learning fatigue" will set in, so don't expect to spend more than an hour or two teaching to roll on any given day. By going longer than this, I can guarantee you that the learning curve will quickly plateau, or even reverse.

OTHER TYPES OF ROLLS

THE OFFSIDE ROLL

An offside roll simply means a roll that you perform on the opposite side from the one you're used to. An offside roll is a good skill to learn because it will further boost your confidence on the water, and through practice, you will become more quickly oriented when upside-down underwater. The offside roll also has some practical uses. When rolling in holes or in surf waves, you have no choice but to roll up on the side of your kayak that faces the breaking wave, which will often be your offside. When paddling in whitewater, you may find your kayak pressed against a rock or caught on an eddy line which forces you to use your offside roll. Another common use for the offside roll is when your natural roll has failed. By recognizing its failure early, you can set up on your offside and use the flipping momentum of your kayak to help you roll up.

The biggest challenge for learning the offside roll is the problem of the "weak side". Just as a learning soccer player has a strong foot and a weak foot, most beginner paddlers discover that they have (or develop) a strong side and weak side. Only dutiful practice on the weak side can change this. Most importantly, practice your hip snap, your draw strokes and your braces on your weak side.

The offset twist (or "feather") of your paddle can also make

Practicing basic hip snap drills on your "weak" side is often all you'll need to develop a strong offside roll.

the offside roll challenging. A paddle that has blades that are offset will require different wrist movements for the natural and offside rolls. During the set-up of a natural roll, the leading arm's wrist will be curled inward somewhat. For a set-up on the offside, the leading arm's wrist will be straight. These differences in your set-up will also change your recovery position. In particular, you'll find that the recovery position for your offside roll means finishing with your wrists aggressively cocked back. With practice, you can figure out the small variances required for the offside roll, but another solution is to start using a paddle with no twist, which is what I do. A paddle with no twist allows your offside roll to be a mirror image of your natural roll, which makes it more intuitive. For whitewater kayakers in particular, there are a number of other good reasons to use a paddle with no twist, and very few good reasons to use a paddle with twist.

THE HAND ROLL

The hand roll is a roll done without the help of a paddle, requiring a highly effective hip snap and careful timing. The hand roll is a great move to master for a number of reasons. Most importantly, it's a confidence booster, and (if you haven't figured it out by now), whitewater kayaking is as much about confidence as it is about skill. Once you learn the hand roll, you might even find that it becomes your preferred roll. Through my first few years of paddling I would sometimes deliberately let go of my paddle underwater and hand roll myself up. I did this is because it was quicker to set-up without the paddle and I knew it was just as reliable. Of course this left me without paddle in the middle of a rapid, but at the time that was a secondary concern. I got by like this in class II and III whitewater, but I knew this approach wasn't going to work as the whitewater got more adventurous and more continuous. The need to roll quickly and reliably—and still keep my paddle—led me to develop my back deck roll technique, but I'll discuss that later on.

I'm going to go over the hand roll with the assumption that you already have a reliable roll. As I did with the C-to-C and sweep rolls, I will break down the hand roll down into three unique parts: the set-up, the catch, and the recovery.

The idea behind the set-up for the hand roll is the same as that for your basic C-to-C and sweep rolls. You need to get your body out as far to the side of the kayak and as close to the surface as possible to maximize the potential of your hip snap. Though the concept is the same, the position of your body is quite different. This position has you leaning out to the side with your head and chest facing downward instead of up towards the sky. Your arms should be up and in front of your face. Most paddlers are stronger rolling up on their right side, which means leaning out to the left with the left arm closest to the bow of the boat.

Now that you're set up, the hand roll can be initiated in one of two ways: by using a two-handed or double-pump technique. These two techniques differ in the same way that the C-to-C and sweep rolls do. The two-handed roll is like the C-to-C roll in that you'll set up to use a single quick and powerful brace from which your hip snap can right the kayak. The double-pump technique uses one arm at a time in a two-step motion that resembles the climbing of a ladder, and which provides longer bracing support just like the sweep roll does. As you may have guessed, you'll probably find the easier of the two techniques to be that which corresponds with the standard style of roll that you prefer. For example, if you're used to getting longer lasting support from a sweep roll, you'll probably prefer the double-pump hand roll. We're going to look at both of these rolls together, because the differences between the two forms are very straightforward.

The key to the catch phase of either roll is to extend out from your set-up position with your hands, arms and body as far out to 90 degrees from your kayak as possible. For the two-handed roll, push downward aggressively with both your hands and arms, and you'll drop your head as you hip snap the boat upright by pulling upward on the trailing knee (the right knee for those rolling up on their right side).

The catch phase for the double-pump technique is slightly different, and in my opinion it is the most effective and reliable hand rolling technique because it gives your hips more time to roll the boat underneath your body, and it forces you to keep your head down throughout the roll. Assuming you're rolling up on your right side, the first step involves pushing down

Setting up for a hand roll.

1 *For a two-handed hand roll, set up with your chest facing downward with the body as close to the surface as possible.*

2 *Push down on the water with one arm after the other.*

3 *As the second arm pushes downward, swing your head and body over the top of the kayak.*

4 *Keep your body as low as possible as you bring it back over the kayak.*

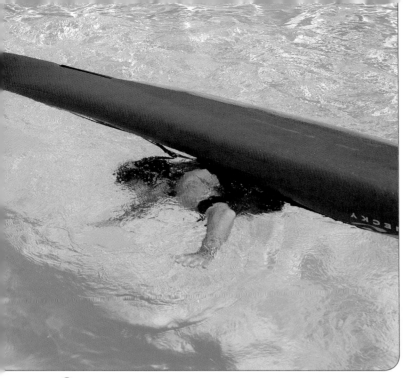

1 For a two-handed hand roll, set up with your chest facing downward with the body as close to the surface as possible.

2 Push both hands downward forcefully at the same time.

3 An explosive hip snap is required to right the kayak, and your head must stay down.

4 Recovering over the back deck of the kayak tends to be easiest for most kayakers.

aggressively on the water with your left hand. This first push draws your body further out to the side and to the surface of the water, while at the same time providing the purchase necessary for your hips to start snapping the boat upright. As soon as this hand begins losing its effectiveness, you'll reach out and push downward with your right hand and continue to rotate the boat upright with your hips. Remember to keep your head down throughout this process. As you begin sweeping downward with your second hand, you've reached the recovery phase of the roll and it's time to swing your body back over top of the kayak.

As with the C-to-C and sweep rolls, there is some debate about whether the ideal recovery position is in leaning forward or backward over your kayak. Again, my preference is to recover over the back deck, for the same reasons: by leaning backward you lower your center of gravity and can roll your hips more easily than you can if you lean forward. Whichever technique you choose, make sure that you keep your body as close to the boat as possible, and leave the head for last!

TRICKS FOR LEARNING THE HAND ROLL

It's tricky to make the transition from a regular roll with the bracing power of a paddle blade to a roll that receives a fraction of the support from only your hands. You can ease this transition while you're learning by using other objects that provide less support than a paddle, but more support than your bare hands. To start, try exchanging your paddle for a PFD or rolled up wetsuit. The flotation will also help draw your hands and body to the surface of the water during the set-up phase. Once you can roll reliably with these in hand, try something smaller and that may not provide additional flotation. In many paddling shops you'll find webbed gloves or hand paddles specifically for this purpose. You can also improvise and use such things as ping pong paddles or shaped pieces of mini-cell foam. Whatever works!

A great way to practice the hand roll is to hold onto a PFD for adding bracing support.

Taking the time to learn advanced rolling techniques like the hand roll will provide a huge boost in confidence and allow you to explore areas that you would have otherwise avoided.

THE BACK DECK ROLL

What I'd always liked about the hand roll was that it was faster than the traditional roll, requiring almost no set up. Of course, as I mentioned in the hand roll section, the major and obvious drawback was that I'd be without a paddle at the end of it! I needed a way to roll just as quickly and reliably but without losing my paddle.

Through playing around and experimenting, I figured out a way to roll across the back deck of my boat. It was fast, reliable and skipped the set-up that other rolls required. I subsequently discovered that the "back deck roll" was a method already known to and in use by others, albeit rarely! I also discovered that my back deck roll technique was slightly different; differing most significantly in that when done

The set-up position for the back deck roll: paddle held low with elbows handing down, forearms horizontal, and wrists cocked back aggressively so that the right paddle blade (for right-handed paddlers) is facing directly down.

correctly it keeps your shoulders safe.

It's not uncommon to hear people comment that though it's a quick roll, it's a dangerous one that leaves a paddler's face exposed, and puts the shoulder at risk. It's true that your face isn't quite as well protected, but you spend a *lot* less time underwater, and your head stays much closer to the surface throughout the roll. Also, for much of the time you are under water, your arms are actually in a very protective position in front of your face. With regard to shoulder safety, there is the potential for the shoulder to be put in an awkward position, but if you keep your hands in front of your body and don't overextend your arms, this roll won't pose any more risk to your shoulder than the standard C-to-C or sweep rolls. So when should you use the back deck roll? I use it almost all the time, and once you master it, it just might become your standard roll as well.

Before I get into describing the roll, there are a few things to note. First, a back deck roll is easiest in short (under 8 feet) whitewater kayaks with low volume (non-bulbous) ends. These features allow the kayak to rotate around your body as much as your body rotates around the kayak. For example, you will find that your stern will be forced underwater during the recovery phase of the roll, which lets you keep your center of gravity lower and leaves more room for error.

Secondly, the back deck roll is an advanced rolling technique that requires good paddle dexterity and a powerful hip snap. Although it's not reserved for expert paddlers, you can expect it to take a while to master—and once you do, you will probably find that it becomes your standard rolling technique. It also provides the foundation for a variety of advanced freestyle kayaking tricks, so if that is an interest of yours, it is well worth the effort.

Because of the right-handed offset on most kayak paddles, it's easiest to perform the back deck roll flipping to the left, with your right blade doing the work. Start with your paddle held low in front of you, with elbows hanging down, forearms held horizontally, and wrists cocked back quite aggressively so that the right paddle blade is facing directly down. You've now formed a rectangle with your arms, paddle and chest. This rectangle should stay relatively intact throughout the roll. Now

1 *Right handed paddlers will find it easiest to roll turning to their left.*

2 *Holding the set-up position of your paddle, lean back and turn your head and body aggressively.*

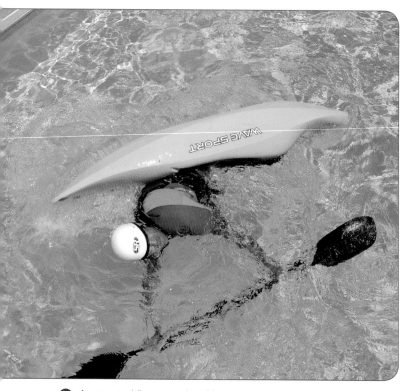

5 *As your paddle sweeps its wide arc, use an aggressive hip snap to roll the boat upright.*

6 *Continue sweeping the paddle in its arc and rolling the kayak with your hip snap. Notice the original set-up position is kept throughout the roll.*

3 Get your right blade into the water as soon as possible because it provides the bracing power.

4 Leaning back and leading with your head, sweep the right blade in an arc over your head with a climbing angle that keeps it near the surface.

7 Swing your body forward as you continue to sweep the paddle to your toes with a climbing angle on the blade.

8 The back deck roll should finish with your body and paddle in a forward position.

1

2

3

4

5

6

COMMON ERRORS FOR THE BACK DECK ROLL

RIGHT BLADE IS NOT ENGAGED EARLY ENOUGH

A common mistake is not engaging the right blade early enough. The right blade should get planted in the water at 90 degrees to the kayak so that you receive bracing support from it as it sweeps up and over your head. If it is not planted at 90 degrees, your paddle will fall over and the right blade won't engage until it is already over your head, losing almost a third of the bracing potential from your paddle. This usually results in starting the hip snap too late, and a failed roll. A common symptom of this error is your body will flop upside-down.

BODY DOESN'T FINISH IN A FORWARD POSITION

If you find yourself finishing the back deck roll lying back and pulling downward on your paddle blade, you're suffering from a common mistake for the back deck roll. Although you can sometimes get away with doing this, your roll will lack fluidity and be prone to failure. This problem is usually a result of an incomplete hip snap relative to the progress of

lean back and aggressively turn your head and upper body to the left. As weird as this sounds (or maybe not for some), think about trying to kiss the stern of your kayak! This keeps your head turned and your neck cocked back. With your head and body aggressively leading the way and your kayak committed to flipping, plant the power face of your right paddle blade in the water as early as possible. Once planted, you'll push your right blade out in a wide arc over your head, and then out to the side and all the way to your toes. If your wrists remain cocked back as they should be, then your right blade will be on a climbing angle that keeps it near the surface and provides the brace your hips need to roll the kayak upright.

If all has gone well to this point, your hips will have snapped your kayak over your head and your head and body will continue to lead the way as your right blade sweeps out to the side of your kayak. The rectangle between your arms, chest, and paddle should remain intact. For the recovery, swing your body forward as you sweep your right blade in an arc to your toes. When your right blade finally reaches your toes, your boat should be completely upright and your body should be in an aggressive forward position, ready for the next stroke.

When watching the best paddlers use their back deck roll, you'll probably notice that their kayaks seem to flip and roll back up in one fluid motion. The key to an ultra-quick back deck roll is committing yourself to flipping once you've passed the point of no return (the point at which no brace will save you efficiently or safely). This commitment involves throwing yourself on the back deck of your kayak and leading the way with your paddle and body. If you can do these two things before you've completely turned upside-down, then you can start the process of rolling yourself upright before your kayak has even finished flipping over!

As Kevin initiates a back deck roll, notice how early his right blade engages the water.

your paddle. If you engaged your right paddle blade at 90 degrees to your kayak in the beginning, and swept that paddle over your head and out to 90 degrees on the other side of your kayak (where you now find yourself) you should have had ample time and support to roll your kayak upright. If you find yourself struggling to roll the kayak upright at this point it means that you either engaged your right blade too late (see the previous error), neglected your hip snap through the early stages of the sweep, or that you didn't have enough climbing angle on your right blade to provide the required support.

LEARNING TIP

Nailing the first successful roll is always the hardest, so you might as well take any advantage you can get. Try using a diving mask or swimming goggles, so you can watch what you are doing.

If you have the correct climbing angle on your paddle blade, the swinging motion of your body from the back deck to the front deck pushes your paddle through the water and provides the leverage for your hips to right the kayak.

Right: A dry roll is exclusive to whitewater kayaks. It requires good back deck roll technique and early commitment to the move.

THE DRY ROLL

If you're rolling a modern whitewater kayak, you can make your back deck roll a dry roll. A dry roll is simply a back deck roll in which you keep your head dry. Does it sound too good to be true? Well, it's not! As you can probably imagine, a dry roll can be a huge asset on steep, shallow creeks or in any other situation where flipping completely upside-down is a bad idea. The key to the dry roll is committing to the roll very early and very quickly. It will also help a great deal if you're using a paddle that has no twist, because it allows you to brace off the water with both of your paddle blades at the same time.

The dry roll is executed in exactly the same way as the standard back deck roll. The only difference is that you'll use

1 *The dry roll starts with the same set-up as the regular back deck roll.*

2 *Engage your right blade in the water early to provide bracing support as quickly as possible.*

3 *Using a paddle with no twist is ideal because it lets you brace against the water with both blades at the same time.*

4 *As the right blade is swept over your head, your hips aggressively snap the stern of your kayak over your head.*

5 *Continue to sweep your right blade out to the side of the kayak with a climbing angle to provide the support necessary to finish the roll.*

6 *To finish the roll, let your body swing to the bow of the kayak while you sweep your paddle to your toes.*

the bracing support from your paddle to hip snap the stern of your kayak completely out of the water and over your head. It is for this reason that the dry roll is limited to modern whitewater kayaks. As the stern rises from the water, the bow will be forced underwater. The shorter your kayak is and the less volume it has, the easier this will be to do. The length and volume in the ends of sea kayaks makes this a virtually impossible feat.

Assuming you're using a paddle with no twist, you'll get your left paddle blade involved at the very beginning of the dry roll. As you commit to the roll by aggressively turning your head and body, you'll plant the power face of your left blade at the stern of your boat. This left blade provides very momentary support that keeps your head above the surface as your boat begins to flip upside-down. As you continue to flip, keep turning your body and get your right blade into the water as quickly as possible. You'll then sweep that blade over your head and out to the side with a climbing angle that keeps it on the surface and provides the bracing power that you'll need to snap the boat up and over your head. As you push your stern into the air and hip snap it over your head, you might also think about pulling your feet down into the water, because the bow of your kayak needs to go down in order for the stern to rise.

If all has gone well, your body will swing into a balanced forward position while you finish sweeping your right blade to your toes. You're now ready for whatever else the river has to throw at you.

THE RE-ENTER AND ROLL

If you've got a roll, but for some reason you miss it and end up swimming, there is a technique for re-entering your kayak while it's upside-down, and then rolling back up. This re-enter and roll technique is really designed for sea kayakers because river kayakers and whitewater kayakers will usually have the much better option of getting to shore where the boat can be emptied and re-entered at a leisurely pace. When sea kayaking, the shore will often be too far away, and even if it can be reached, it will likely be steep, rugged and subject to crashing waves that will make getting out a nightmare if not impossible altogether.

As I see it, the re-enter and roll is a technique that should never be necessary. If you don't have a bombproof roll, you should always paddle with other people who can offer an assisted rescue. If you do have a strong roll and choose to paddle alone, you should be a capable enough paddler that you won't swim unless confronted with unexpectedly challenging conditions. If for some reason you do end up swimming as a lone but competent paddler, the conditions that resulted in your swim will also make the re-enter and roll an incredibly difficult and unreliable maneuver. With all this said, the ocean is a strange and dynamic environment where any number of situations can arise, and where rescue situations can at any time become life threatening. Any edge that you can give yourself is well potentially worth taking the time to practice and could very well make a huge difference some day.

The trick to the re-enter and roll is getting your butt into the seat and your knees comfortably in place under the thigh hooks. Only then will you be able to hip snap your boat upright. Once your knees and butt are positioned, you can use your natural roll to right the kayak, but a sweep roll will definitely work best because a kayak filled with water tends to roll very slowly. Once you've rolled the boat upright, you'll need to pump the water out, or you could make a dash for shore and empty the water there. By missing your roll in the first place, it probably means that your roll isn't as strong as it could be, and that you could use the help of a paddle float. Attach a paddle float to the blade that you'll use to brace with, and you'll get a lot more support for your roll. Once you're upright, the paddle float will also give you a good brace to use while pumping the water out of your water.

1 & **2** *Holding onto your paddle with one hand, grab the cockpit coaming and slide yourself into the kayak.*

3 & **4** *Get settled into the seat with your legs under the thigh hooks and then assume your regular set-up position.*

5 & **6** *Use your favored rolling technique to right the kayak and prepare to pump the water out.*

THE CROWD PLEASER

The warm temperatures and the long stretches of flat water on the Ottawa River make it the perfect place for learning fun kayak tricks that have absolutely no practical value. The Crowd Pleaser is one of my favorites. It is wonderfully useless and highly entertaining. This one was developed during the long hours I spent as a safety kayaker, waiting for rafts to come downstream.

1 *Get the paddle spinning in the palms of your hands.*

2 *Toss the paddle straight up and flip upside-down.*

5 *Pass the paddle over the hull of your boat to your left hand.*

6 *Spin the paddle in your left hand as you hand roll up with your right hand.*

3 Cross your fingers (on your left hand) and hope to catch the paddle with your right hand.

4 Catch the paddle.

7 Keep your body as close to the boat as possible.

8 Humbly accept the applause from the crowd.

CHAPTER 5

ROLLING IN ROUGH WATER

ROLLING IN CURRENT

ROLLING IN HOLES

ROLLING IN OCEAN SURF

The only way to get comfortable rolling in current is to practice.

I was taught early on that in rough water, good paddling technique is as important as having strong paddling muscles. What I wasn't taught right away is that kayaking is as much a mental game as it is a physical one. In order to improve, you need to develop both sides. Assuming that you have developed a confident and reliable flat water roll, your biggest challenge for rolling in rough water conditions is to develop your mental game and not let yourself be rushed when you find yourself upside-down in churning waters.

Just like the physical elements of rolling, it takes practice to develop your mental game, and this can be done in stages. A great way to start is to practice rolling in flat water after establishing forward speed. Flipping as you're moving forward helps imitate the forces you'll feel from waves or current, and you can start by setting up just before you flip so that you're already in position. When you're comfortable doing this, try the same thing without setting up before flipping. In fact, try it flipping in as many different positions as you can so that it

becomes second nature to have to assume your set-up position when upside-down.

The next step for whitewater kayakers, or for sea kayakers who plan to paddle in tidal currents, is to practice flipping and rolling in current. Of course, you'll want to do so in light current and deep water. You can start by flipping in your set-up position, but ultimately you'll want to practice rolling in current without setting up beforehand. Once you're comfortable doing this, it's time to start playing around and allowing yourself to flip more unexpectedly. A great skill for both whitewater and sea kayakers to practice is backward eddy turns. Another one for whitewater kayakers to practice at this stage is the eddy line stern squirt. Not only can you expect to flip when practicing them, but they are great skills to develop.

Now that you're starting to get control of your mental game, let's take a look at specific rough water situations that you'll encounter.

ROLLING IN CURRENT

Rolling in current can be tricky at times. The first thing to know is that the most difficult place to roll a kayak is on an eddy line. Eddy lines have unpredictable currents that can make it difficult to get the paddle into a decent set-up position, or even to get good purchase on the water with your bracing blade. If you find yourself caught upside-down on an eddy line and are having trouble rolling, you're usually best off to relax, be patient, and wait a few seconds. Unless you are caught in a particularly powerful eddy, you'll likely drift downstream. The water will be calmer, the eddy line will get progressively weaker and wider, and rolling will be easier.

Rolling in the main current is generally a lot more straightforward. If you think about it, when you're floating in current, you're moving at the same speed as the water. This means that the water is effectively still, relative to your kayak, and that rolling in current is no different than rolling in flat water. If you're paddling downstream faster than the current, or have just peeled out of an eddy into the current and have not yet reached the same speed as the water, you'll feel the water tugging at your body and paddle when you flip over. This will only last momentarily as you are accelerated or decelerated to the same speed as the current. The best paddlers will actually use these forces to help their roll, but for most paddlers, the best option is to relax and take the time to set-up the roll correctly.

PERFORMANCE TIP

Big water often has powerful secondary currents which can pull the paddle underwater during the set-up phase of the C-to-C roll. For this reason, whitewater kayakers paddling on large volume rivers, or sea kayakers paddling in large volume tidal rips, generally have more success with a sweep roll than with the C-to-C roll.

ROLLING IN HOLES

Rolling in a hole can be either one of the easiest things to do, or it can be virtually impossible. It all depends on which side of the boat you're trying to roll up on. If you're trying to roll up on the upstream side of the boat, you might as well give up! You're not going to get anywhere. On the other hand, if you are setting up on the downstream side, then there's a good chance you'll be upright before you know it. The reason is that the green water rushing under the foam pile can hit the power face of your paddle and literally push you upright with minimal hip snap involved.

You might even have seen someone unintentionally do a full revolution in a hole (otherwise referred to as "window shading"). This happens when a paddler is rolled upright more quickly than was expected, with the help of the hole. For a true window shade, the stunned paddler then catches their upstream edge and gets flipped right back upside-down!

Since it is imperative that you roll up on the downstream side of your kayak, it's not up to you whether you roll up on your natural side or on your offside. This is why it's a good idea to develop an offside roll before you go playing around in holes.

ROLLING IN OCEAN SURF

Performing a rescue in the ocean's surf zone can be one of the most demanding situations. For this reason, if you're playing around in surf, you really should have a reliable roll. Being upside-down in surf can be very disorienting, because when a wave passes over top of you, the water will tug your body in all directions. If you feel this happening in small- or moderately-sized surf, try to relax while upside-down. It usually won't take long before the wave passes you by and the water calms down. In bigger surf, you can't rely on the wave passing over top of you, so you'll need to learn to roll in waves. Rolling in a breaking ocean wave is no different than rolling a hole. You need to roll up on the breaking side of the wave. If you're set-up on the correct side of your kayak, it can be incredibly easy because the wave will help roll you upright. But if you're set up on the wrong side, you'll be fighting an impossible battle and will need to move to the set-up position on the other side of your kayak. Of course, the trick is to get really good at orienting yourself while underwater so that you know which side is which, and this only comes with practice.

A good trick that can save you the time of having to feel for the position of your blade is to place an index on the control handgrip of your paddle. This index can be a small strip of foam or wood that is taped to your paddle shaft so that it fits under the fingers of your control hand. Over time, you'll be able to recognize when your hand positioning is off just by the feel of the index. Many paddles now have built-in indexes or oval shafts, which serve the same purpose.

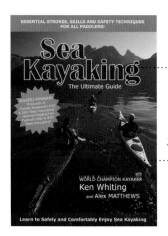
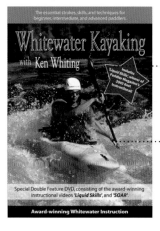
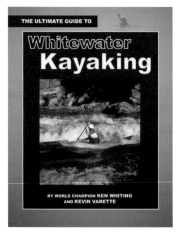
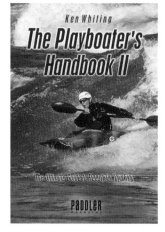